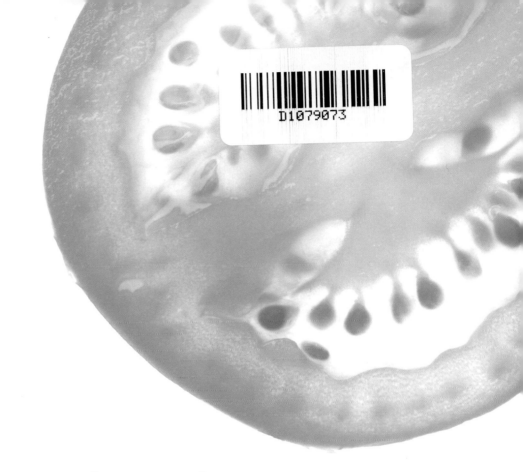

No-Check
Low-Check 2

Contents

No-Check Soups

Bortch	7
Broccoli & Tarragon	8
Three Tomato	9
Chicken & Celery	10
Carrot & Chilli	11
Sweet & Sour	11
Marrow & Mint	12
Curried Butternut Squash	13

No-Check Sides & Salads

Cucumber, Tomato & Onion Salsa	19	Carrot & Courgette Noodles	22
Garlic & Herb Dressing/Dip	19	Strawberry Chutney	23
Greens & Citrus Salad	20	Peppered Swede Mash	24
Artichoke Heart & Tomato Salad	20	Cauliflower Mash	24
Spanish-style Mixed Salad	21	Turnip & Parsley Mash	25
Roasted Four Pepper Salad	21	Celeriac & Lemon Mash	25
Leek & Green Bean Noodles	22		

No-Check Starters

Mighty Mushrooms	15
Aubergine & Red Pepper Pâté	16
Courgettes Provençale	17

Make a Meal of it!

Mushroom Stroganoff	27
Vegetable Chilli	28
Simple Vegetable Korma	29
Stuffed Aubergine	30
Egg White Omelette	31

No-Check Drinks & Desserts

Rhubarb & Ginger Ale Smoothie	33
Peach Smoothie	33
Mint Tea	34
Fresh Lemonade	34
Sweet Spiced Squash	35
Jelly Foam	36
Pink Cloud	37

Just **One Check**

Just One Check Foods   **39**

Low-Check Recipes

up to 6 Checks

Sausages in Red Wine Gravy	**41**
Normandy Pork	**42**
Honey, Lemon & Garlic Turkey	**43**
Fisherman's Stew	**45**
Vegetable & Pasta Lunch Bowl	**46**
Pasta Brunch	**47**
Orange & Soy Quorn Fillets	**48**
Vegetable Spring Rolls	**49**
Corned Beef & Hoisin Wrappers	**50**
Spanish Tuna Salad	**51**

Low-Check Main Meals

up to 12 Checks

Red Pesto Chicken with Pan-fried Courgettes & New Potatoes	**53**
Microwave Meatloaf & Mash	**54**
Beef Chow Mein	**55**
Tagliatelle with Ham, Peas & Crème Fraîche	**57**
Chicken & Potato Curry	**58**
Top Tapas	**59**
Steamed Sweet Chilli Fish & Noodles	**60**
Fish & Prawn Pie	**61**
Spicy Chickpeas & Couscous	**63**

Low-Check Sweet Treats

Quick Strawberry Trifle	**65**
Ambassador's Choice	**65**
Brandied Apricots	**66**
Honeyed Figs	**66**
Apple Snow	**67**
Jelly with Orange Cream	**68**
Alaska Special	**69**
Prune & Apple Muffins	**71**
Sultana Scones	**72**
No-added-fat Sponge	**73**

No-Check **Low-Check** Foods

No-Check Vegetables	**75**	No-Check Dressings & Sauces	**79**
No-Check Additions	**78**	No-Check Pickles	**79**
No-Check Drinks	**78**	Low-Check Best Buys	**80**

You loved our first No-Check Low-Check book - so by popular demand, here is the sequel!

We all know that following the Scottish Slimmers' Positive Eating Plan means you can enjoy all types of food - without feeling guilty. But, we also know that some foods do have a high Check value, and if we want to stay in control, there has to be some compensation should we over-indulge now and again.

As before, No-Check Low-Check 2 is full of tasty ideas that make the most of No-Check foods, Every Day Bonus foods and other foods which have a low Check value. Eat at any time but, on average, keep within your daily Checks allowance.

Although most of us have our usual routine, spending approximately the same amount on our normal meals and snacks each day, there are frequently times when we need to cut back a little -

• Calories Checks Fat Grams

All values exclude "No-Check " foods which do not need to be counted.

- If you are trying to save Checks for a special social occasion, these recipes provide nutrition and satisfaction but make it easy to save.

- **Had a bad day or two? There's no need to starve in order to try and compensate. Just make yourself a couple of nice low-Check meals, then get back to your usual weight loss routine.**

- These recipes may be low on Checks, but they're high on taste, nutrition and satisfaction. You can be reassured that many of the foods used - such as vegetables, fruit, lean meat and fish - are packed full of beneficial nutrients that can help you feel good whilst doing you a power of good.

- **We've also included lists of No-Check and Low-Check basic foods ideal for using in your own healthy meal ideas. Losing weight, and keeping it off, will be much easier if you get to know these foods well and build meals around them.**

- Positive Eating allows for the fact that "No-Check" foods do contain a few calories, but we've taken them into account when recommending daily Check allowances. So, as far as you're concerned, if it has "No-Check" value, you don't need to count it!

No-Check Recipes

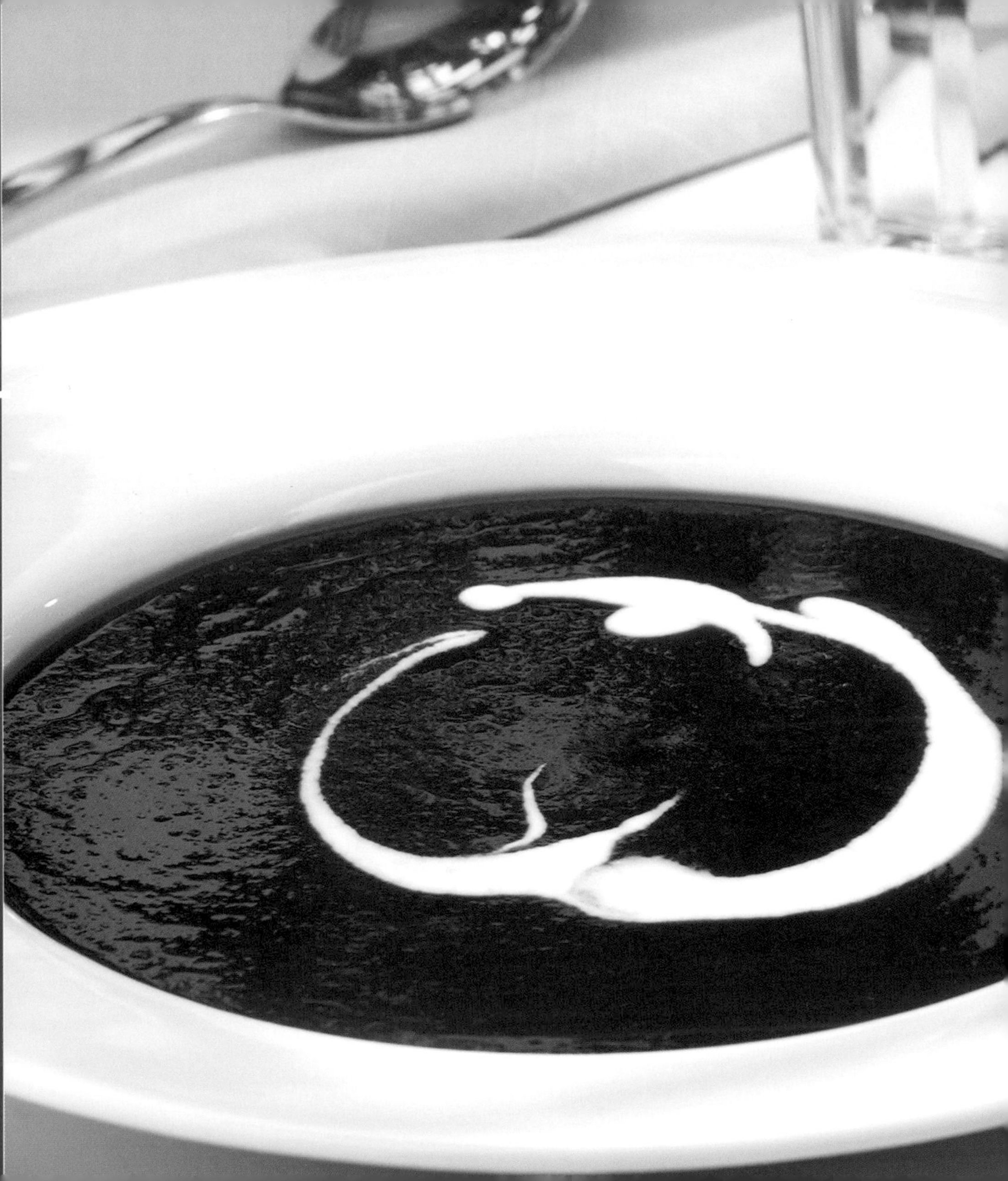

■ Bortch

using Every Day Bonus milk*

- 600ml/1 pint beef stock
- 250g pack cooked and peeled beetroot (no vinegar), roughly chopped
- 1 medium onion, chopped
- 115g/4 oz savoy cabbage, shredded
- 300-450ml/½-¾ pint warm water
- Black pepper
- 1 rounded tbsp low-fat natural yoghurt per serving

Put stock into a large saucepan and bring to the boil.

Add beetroot and onion, cover and simmer 10 minutes. Add cabbage and cook covered a further 10 minutes.

Allow to cool a little, then transfer to a liquidiser and blend gradually adding about 300-450ml/½-¾ pint extra warm water, until smooth and velvety.

Re-heat gently and season with black pepper.

Swirl 1 rounded tbsp low-fat natural yoghurt into each serving.

1 rounded tbsp low-fat natural yoghurt is the equivalent of one-quarter of Every Day Bonus milk/yoghurt allowance.

If not using Every Day Bonus allowance, count 1 Check per 1 rounded tbsp low-fat natural yoghurt.

■ Broccoli & Tarragon Soup

No-Check Food

Courtesy of member Bernadine Dooley, Clydebank

- **2 medium onions, chopped**
- **2 cloves garlic, crushed**
- **Spray oil**
- **450g/1lb broccoli florets**
- **1 tbsp fresh tarragon leaves or 1 tsp dried**
- **1 bay leaf**
- **600ml/1 pint vegetable stock**

Put onions and garlic into a large oil-sprayed saucepan. Cover and cook gently about 10 minutes until softened. Stir occasionally and add a little water if necessary to prevent sticking.

Add broccoli, tarragon, bay leaf and stock, bring to a simmer, cover and cook until all ingredients are soft.

Allow to cool a little, remove bay leaf and liquidise. Re-heat as necessary.

■ Three Tomato Soup

- **30g/1 oz dried sun-dried tomatoes (e.g. Merchant Gourmet)**
- **250g/9 oz fresh tomatoes**
- **2 x 400g cans plum tomatoes**
- **1 medium onion, chopped**
- **1 clove garlic, crushed**
- **Spray oil**
- **150ml/¼ pint vegetable stock**
- **2 tsp granulated sweetener**
- **A few fresh basil leaves, finely shredded**

Snip the sun-dried tomatoes into small pieces, cover with a little boiling water and leave to hydrate 10-15 minutes.

Pour boiling water over fresh tomatoes and leave 2-3 minutes. Remove carefully, peel, de-seed and chop roughly.

Soften onions and garlic in pan sprayed with oil. Add canned tomatoes, bring to a simmer and cook gently 10 minutes, stirring now and again. Allow to cool a little, then liquidise until smooth. Pass through a sieve to remove seeds and return to pan.

Stir in sun-dried tomatoes with liquid, fresh tomatoes, stock and sweetener. Heat gently and serve garnished with finely shredded basil.

Chicken & Celery Soup

No-Check Food

1 0xo chicken cube
300ml/½ pint water
1 large stick celery, finely sliced

Crumble cube into a small saucepan, add water and bring to the boil, stirring until cube has dissolved.

Add celery and simmer approximately 15 minutes or until tender. Add more water, if liquid reduces too much.

■ Carrot & Chilli Soup

- **450g/1lb carrots, sliced**
- **175g/6 oz onions, chopped**
- **1 medium red chilli, de-seeded and sliced**
- **900ml/1½ pints chicken or vegetable stock**
- **Lime wedges (optional)**

Put carrots, onions, chilli and stock into a large saucepan. Bring to the boil, then cover and simmer about 15 minutes, or until carrots are tender.

Allow to cool a little, then blend until smooth.

Re-heat as necessary and, if liked, serve with a squeeze of lime juice.

■ Sweet & Sour Soup

using Every Day Bonus fruit*

Courtesy of member Agnes Latta, Bathgate

- **400g can tomatoes, chopped**
- **1 small onion, chopped**
- **8 ready-to-eat dried apricots, chopped**
- **½ tsp cumin**
- **600ml/1 pint chicken or vegetable stock**

Place all ingredients into a saucepan. Bring to the boil, then simmer gently 30 minutes.

Allow to cool a little then blend until smooth.

May be served hot or cold.

* One-quarter of the recipe uses half of one average serving Every Day Bonus fruit.

If not using Every Day Bonus fruit, count 1 Check per one-quarter of the recipe.

■ Marrow & Mint Soup

- **1 medium marrow, peeled, de-seeded and chopped**
- **1 medium onion, chopped**
- **Good handful fresh mint leaves**
- **2 Oxo vegetable cubes**
- **600ml/1 pint hot water**

Place marrow, onions and mint in a large saucepan. Dissolve vegetable cubes in hot water and add to pan. Bring to a simmer, cover and cook approximately 15 minutes, or until vegetables are soft.

Allow to cool a little and liquidise for just a few seconds. Re-heat as necessary.

■ Curried Butternut Squash Soup

No-Check Food

Courtesy of Class Assistant Jaqui McIntosh, Edinburgh

- **1 medium butternut squash, peeled and cubed**
- **2 medium onions, chopped**
- **2 sticks celery, sliced**
- **2 cloves garlic, crushed**
- **1 tbsp curry powder, or to taste**
- **1 Oxo chicken or vegetable cube**

Place all ingredients in a large saucepan and cover with water. Bring to the boil, then cover and simmer until vegetables are soft, stirring now and again.

Allow to cool a little then liquidise until smooth, adding a little extra water if necessary.

Best if left a few hours for flavours to develop. Re-heat gently.

No-Check Starters

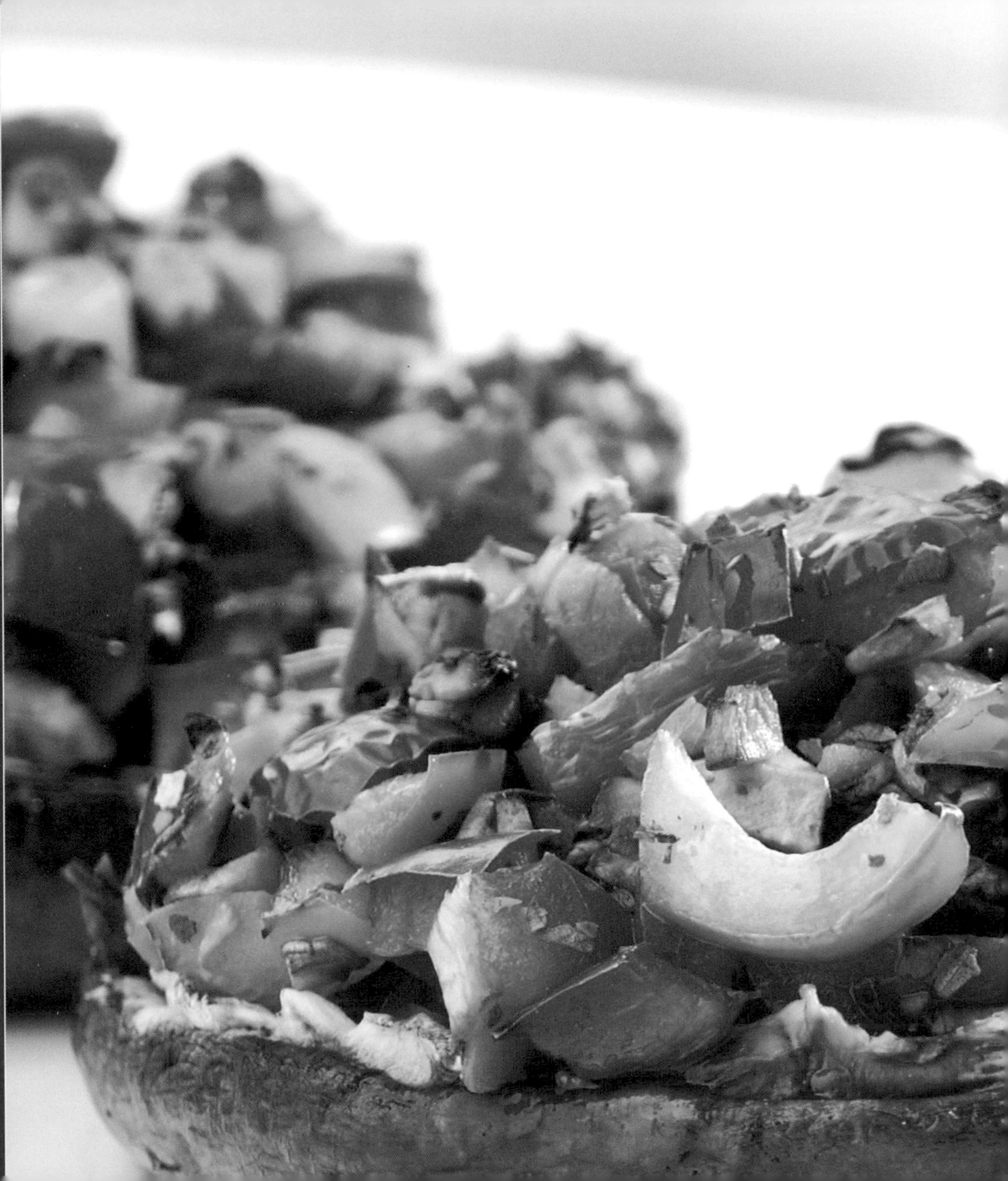

■ Mighty Mushrooms

- 45g/1½ oz frozen mixed peppers
- 2 button mushrooms, finely chopped
- 1 small clove garlic, finely chopped
- 1 small tomato, chopped
- Small pinch dried oregano or thyme
- Salt and black pepper
- 2 large "saucer" (Portobello) mushrooms
- Spray oil, preferably olive oil flavour

Pre-heat oven to 220°C/gas mark 8.

Allow peppers to defrost a little and cut into dice, if not already chopped. Put in a sieve and rinse under cold water to defrost completely. Drain on kitchen paper.

Mix peppers with chopped mushrooms, garlic, tomato and herbs. Season to taste.

Spray white side of "saucer" mushrooms with oil, turn over and pile mixture on top. Place on a non-stick baking tray and bake approximately 15-20 minutes, until juices start to run.

■ Aubergine & Red Pepper Pâté

- 1 aubergine, approximately 300-400g/10-14 oz
- 1 medium red pepper, approximately 150g/5 oz
- 2 cloves garlic
- 1 dspn finely chopped parsley
- Salt and black pepper

Pre-heat oven to 220°C/gas mark 8.

Remove stalks from aubergine and pepper and cut in half lengthways. De-seed pepper. Wrap garlic cloves in foil. Place aubergines and peppers cut-side down on a non-stick baking tray together with garlic. Bake approximately 30-35 minutes until aubergines start to collapse and pepper skins are blistered and charred.

Place peppers in a polythene bag 10 minutes to steam, then peel and dice flesh.

When cool enough to handle, place aubergines in a sieve over a bowl and press out bitter juices with a spoon. Scoop aubergine flesh away from skin into a blender. Squeeze in garlic cloves releasing softened flesh. Blend in a few short bursts, mixing with a fork in between. Consistency should be fairly smooth.

Transfer aubergine to a bowl and stir in diced peppers, chopped parsley and seasoning to taste. Serve at room temperature.

Above quantity is enough for 2 good servings as a starter. If doubling quantities for 4, oven time may be a bit longer.

■ Courgettes Provençale

- **1 onion, finely chopped**
- **1-2 cloves garlic, crushed**
- **Spray oil**
- **400g can chopped tomatoes**
- **1 tsp red wine vinegar**
- **½ tsp Herbes de Provence**
- **4 medium courgettes, sliced thickly**
- **Salt and black pepper**

Place onions and garlic in a medium saucepan sprayed with oil. Cover and cook gently until soft, stirring frequently.

Add tomatoes, red wine vinegar and herbs. Bring to the boil and stir in courgettes. Cover and simmer gently approximately 15 minutes, or until courgettes are tender. Season to taste (may not be necessary).

Serve either hot or cold (at room temperature).

No-Check Sides & Salads

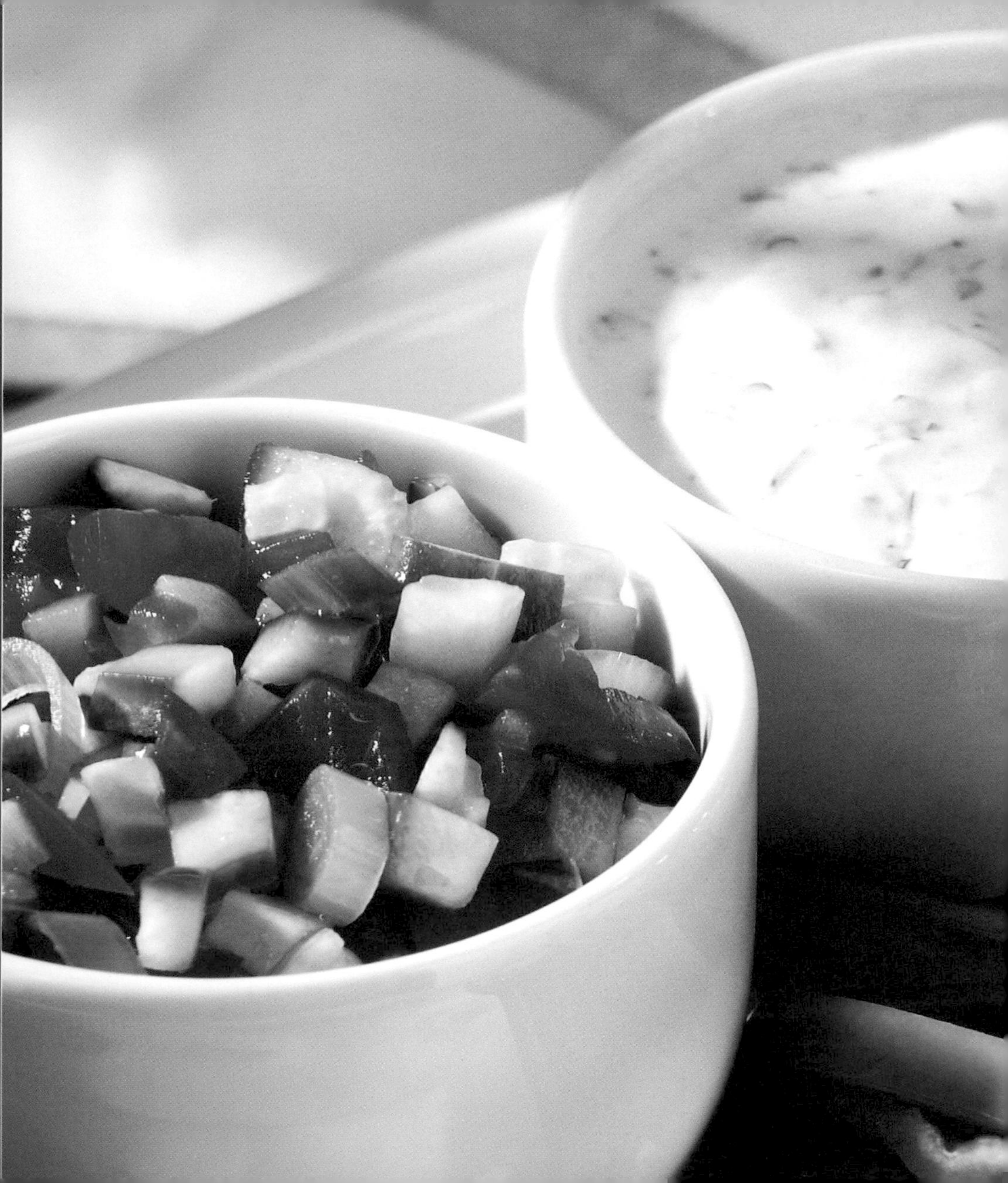

Cucumber, Tomato & Onion Salsa

No-Check Food

- **5cm/2" cucumber**
- **2 tomatoes**
- **1-2 spring onions**
- **Salt and black pepper**
- **1 tbsp lemon juice**
- **½ tsp Worcester sauce**
- **½ tsp granulated sweetener**

Cut the cucumber and tomatoes into small dice. Slice the spring onions. Mix all in a bowl together with any juices. Season to taste.

Mix together the lemon juice, Worcester sauce and sweetener and stir well into vegetables. Best if covered and left to marinate 30 minutes before serving, stirring once or twice.

Garlic & Herb Dressing/Dip

No-Check Food

using Every Day Bonus milk*

- **100g fat-free fromage frais**
- **2 good pinches garlic powder, or to taste**
- **Good pinch of salt**
- **¼ tsp granulated sweetener**
- **1 dspn finely chopped fresh parsley**

Stir the garlic powder, salt and sweetener into the fromage frais and mix well. Stir in the chopped parsley.

The whole recipe is equivalent to half your Every Day Bonus milk allowance.

If not using Every Day Bonus milk, count 2 Checks for the whole recipe.

■ Greens & Citrus Salad

using Every Day Bonus fruit*

- **30g/1 oz prepared mixed dark salad leaves, including baby spinach leaves and/or watercress**
- **1 satsuma or tangerine**
- **1 small trimmed spring onion**
- **Lemon juice**
- **Black pepper**

Arrange salad leaves on serving plate or side-salad bowl. Peel and segment the satsuma or tangerine and arrange on salad leaves.

Finely slice the spring onion and scatter over salad. Sprinkle with plenty of lemon juice and season with black pepper.

Good served as a side dish with spicy foods.

* Whole recipe uses half of one average serving Every Day Bonus fruit.
If not using Every Day Bonus fruit, count 1 Check for the whole recipe.

■ Artichoke Heart & Tomato Salad

- **400g can artichoke hearts**
- **12 baby plum tomatoes or cherry tomatoes**
- **Balsamic vinegar**

Drain artichoke hearts into a sieve and rinse well under cold running water. Cut into quarters.

Halve baby plum tomatoes and mix with artichokes.

Serve out required amount and sprinkle with a few drops balsamic vinegar.

■ Spanish-style mixed salad

Coutesey of Class Assistant Jaqui McIntosh, Edinburgh

- **Lettuce leaves, shredded**
- **Red onion, chopped,**
- **Red pepper, chopped**
- **Carrot, grated,**
- **Tomato, chopped,**
- **Cooked asparagus, chopped**
- **Kraft Fat-Free Italian Dressing**

Use as much of each ingredient as appropriate for your needs and mix all ingredients together.

■ Roasted Four Pepper Salad

- **1 red pepper**
- **1 green pepper**
- **1 orange pepper**
- **1 yellow pepper**
- **A little rocket or pretty salad leaves for garnish**
- **Balsamic vinegar**

Pre-heat oven to 220°C/gas mark 8.

Remove stalk and seeds from peppers and cut into quarters. Place skin-side-up on a large baking tray. Roast in the hottest part of the oven approximately 30-40 minutes, or until skins are blistered and charred.

Put peppers in a polythene bag 10 minutes to steam. Remove, peel and allow to cool.

For each serving, arrange 1 piece of each colour pepper on a serving plate, garnished with a few salad leaves. Sprinkle with a little balsamic vinegar.

■ Leek & Green Bean Noodles

No-Check Food

Use approximately equal amounts of leeks and green beans.

Thoroughly clean leek(s) by cutting through the centre lengthways and washing under running water. Cut into narrow strips.

Cook frozen sliced green beans in boiling water approximately 3 minutes. Add leek strips and cook a further 2 minutes.

Drain and either serve as a vegetable accompaniment, or top with low-fat pasta sauce (counting Checks in sauce as appropriate), or your own no-Check sauce made from onions, tomatoes and herbs.

■ Carrot & Courgette Noodles

No-Check Food

Use a vegetable peeler to cut long thin strips of courgette and carrot.

Place in boiling water and cook about 1 minute until just tender.

Drain and either serve hot as a vegetable accompaniment, or allow to cool and serve as a salad dressed with oil-free vinaigrette.

■ Strawberry Chutney

using Every Day Bonus fruit*

- **150g/5 oz strawberries**
- **1 tbsp balsamic vinegar**
- **1½ tbsp water**
- **½ tsp black pepper, or to taste**

Slice washed and hulled strawberries and place in a saucepan with remaining ingredients.

Cook uncovered over low heat approximately 25 minutes, stirring occasionally, until thickened.

Transfer to a covered container, cool and refrigerate.

The whole recipe uses one average serving Every Day Bonus fruit.

If not using Every Day Bonus fruit, count 2 Checks for the whole recipe. Or for practical purposes, count half a Check for a serving of about one-sixth to one-quarter of the recipe.

No-Check Food

■ Peppered Swede Mash

No-Check Food

Peel, chop and boil orange swede/turnip until soft. Or use half swede/turnip and half carrot.

Drain, reserving cooking liquid. Mash vegetables and use some of the cooking liquid if too stiff, or some skimmed milk from Every Day Bonus allowance.

Season with a little salt and plenty of coarsely ground black pepper.

Variation

Use pumpkin or butternut squash as an alternative to orange swede/turnip.

■ Cauliflower Mash

No-Check Food

Boil cauliflower until soft. Mash lightly with a fork and season to taste. Can be used as a no-Check alternative to mashed potato or rice.

Variation

For Spiced Cauliflower Mash, make as above. Stir in some cumin, a tiny pinch at a time, according to taste, and serve sprinkled with a little garam masala. Use as an accompaniment to Middle Eastern dishes or curries.

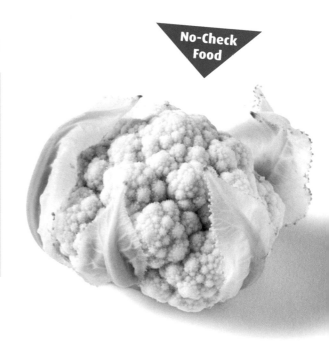

■ Turnip & Parsley Mash

Peel, chop and boil white turnip until soft.

Drain, reserving cooking liquid. Mash using a little of the liquid or some skimmed milk from Every Day Bonus allowance.

Season to taste with salt and pepper and stir in some finely chopped parsley.

■ Celeriac & Lemon Mash

Peel and chop celeriac. Plunge into boiling water and boil until soft, about 10 minutes.

Drain, reserving cooking liquid. Mash, using a little of the liquid.

Stir in finely grated lemon zest, using about 1 tsp per 250-300g/9-10 oz peeled weight.

Season to taste with salt, pepper and a good squeeze of lemon juice.

No-Check Make a Meal of it!

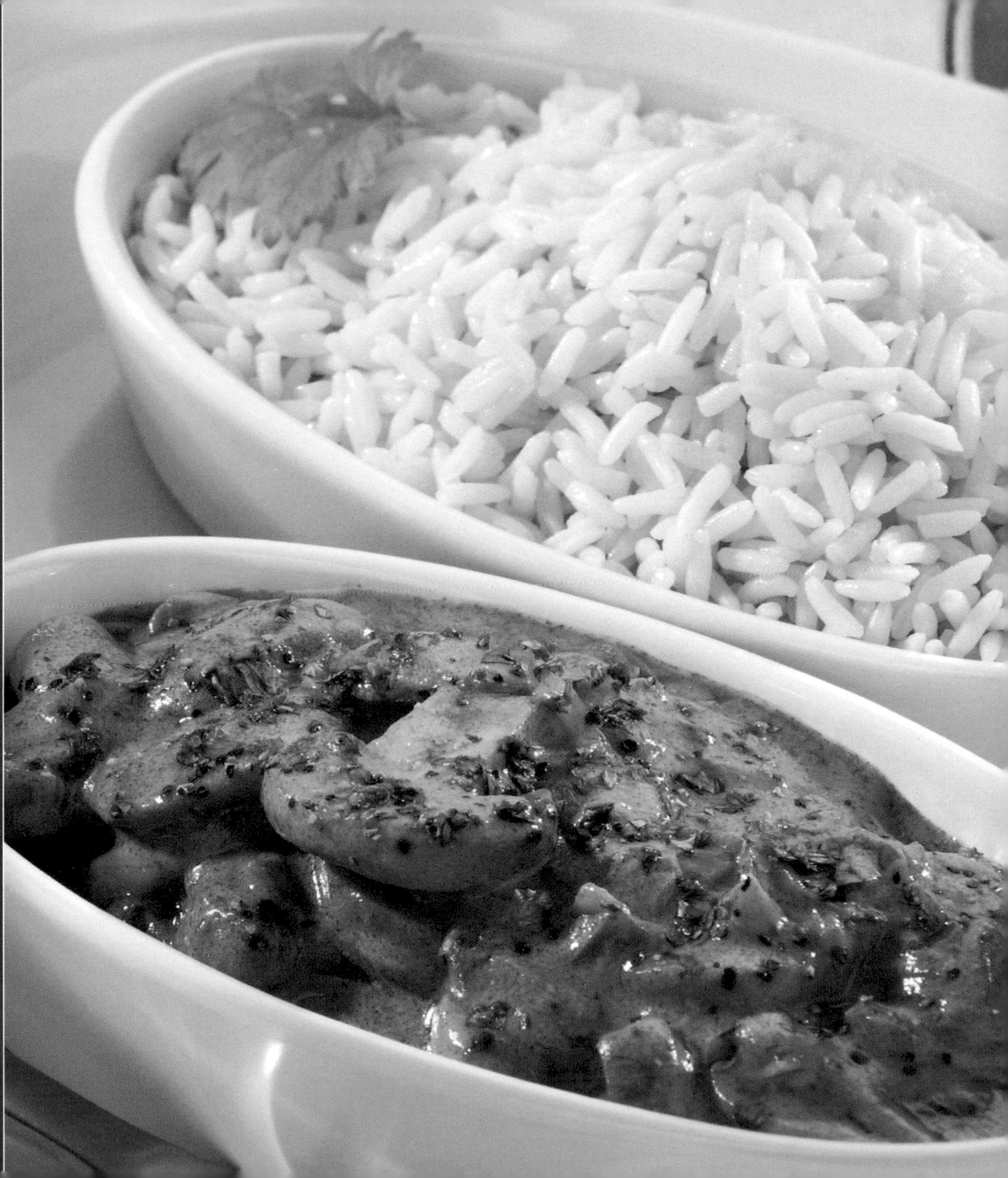

■ Mushroom Stroganoff

using Every Day Bonus milk*

- **1 small onion, chopped**
- **Spray oil**
- **115g/4 oz mushrooms, roughly chopped**
- **1 Oxo vegetable cube**
- **1 dspn tomato purée**
- **Pinch of thyme**
- **100g/2 heaped tbsp fat-free natural fromage frais**
- **Black pepper**
- **1 dspn chopped fresh parsley**

Cook onions gently in pan sprayed with oil until softened and starting to brown. Add 1-2 tbsp water, if necessary, to prevent sticking.

Add mushrooms, crumbled vegetable cube, tomato purée and thyme. Stir 1 minute. Add 100ml/3½ fl.oz hot water and simmer gently 3-4 minutes.

Remove pan from heat and stir in fromage frais. Return to heat and warm gently stirring for a few seconds. Sprinkle with black pepper and chopped parsley.

Either serve on it's own or add a portion of rice or mashed potatoes for a more substantial meal (counting Checks as appropriate).

Fromage frais used in recipe is the equivalent of half of Every Day Bonus milk/yoghurt allowance.

If not using Every Day Bonus allowance, count 2 Checks for the whole recipe.

■ Vegetable Chilli

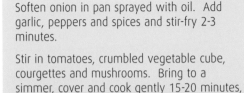

- **1 onion, sliced**
- **Spray oil**
- **1 clove garlic, crushed**
- **150g/5 oz frozen sliced mixed peppers**
- **1 tsp chilli powder, or to taste**
- **Good pinch cumin**
- **400g can tomatoes**
- **½ Oxo vegetable cube**
- **1 courgette, sliced**
- **3 mushrooms, roughly chopped**

Soften onion in pan sprayed with oil. Add garlic, peppers and spices and stir-fry 2-3 minutes.

Stir in tomatoes, crumbled vegetable cube, courgettes and mushrooms. Bring to a simmer, cover and cook gently 15-20 minutes, stirring occasionally.

Variation

For a more substantial meal, rinsed and drained canned kidney beans can be added with the courgettes and mushrooms.

Count 1 Check per rounded tbsp kidney beans.

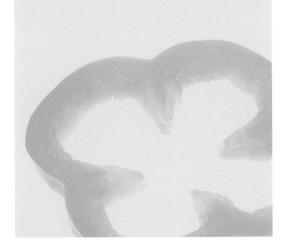

■ Simple Vegetable Korma

using Every Day Bonus milk *

- **1 small onion, chopped**
- **Spray oil**
- **1 clove garlic, crushed**
- **1 dspn korma curry powder, or other mild curry powder**
- **115g/4 oz cauliflower florets**
- **115g/4 oz carrots, peeled and sliced**
- **150ml/¼ pint chicken or vegetable stock**
- **115g/4 oz frozen sliced green beans**
- **2 heaped tbsp diet natural yoghurt or 0% fat Greek yoghurt**

Cook onion gently in a medium saucepan sprayed with oil until soft and starting to colour. Add garlic and curry powder and stir over gentle heat 1 minute.

Add cauliflower, carrots and stock. Bring to a simmer, cover and cook 20 minutes, stirring occasionally. Add green beans, return to a simmer, cover and cook 5 minutes more.

Remove from heat, leave for 1 minute then tilt pan and stir yoghurt well into juices. Mix sauce through vegetables.

* Yoghurt used in recipe is the equivalent of half of Every Day Bonus milk/yoghurt allowance.

If not using Every Day Bonus allowance, count 2 Checks for the whole recipe.

■ Stuffed Aubergine

- **1 medium aubergine**
- **1 onion, chopped**
- **1 medium carrot, diced,**
- **1 medium stick celery, finely sliced**
- **1 tbsp tomato purée**
- **Pinch of mixed herbs**
- **Salt and pepper**

Pre-heat oven to 200°C/gas mark 6.

Cut aubergine in half lengthways. Scoop out and retain centres, leaving 2 "shells". Sprinkle inside of shells lightly with salt and place cut-side down on a baking tray. Bake 20 minutes.

Meanwhile, plunge onion, carrot, celery and chopped flesh removed from centre of aubergine into boiling water, then cover and cook at a gentle boil approximately 15 minutes until softened. Drain vegetables, roughly mash with a fork and stir in tomato purée and herbs. If necessary, season lightly with salt and pepper (celery and tomato purée add a lot of flavour, often making it unnecessary to add salt).

Remove shells from oven, turn over and fill with vegetable mixture. Return to oven 15 minutes, until aubergine is soft.

Variation

After filling with vegetable mixture, on each half, sprinkle over 1 tbsp fresh wholemeal breadcrumbs and 1 tsp grated parmesan cheese. Bake until crumbs are golden, about 15-20 minutes. Count 2 Checks for the whole recipe.

■ Egg-White Omelette

- **3 button mushrooms, sliced**
- **1 tomato, chopped**
- **Spray oil**
- **2 medium egg whites**
- **Pinch of salt**
- **Spray oil**

Cook mushrooms and tomatoes in a non-stick pan sprayed with oil. Remove from pan and keep warm.

Beat egg whites until just foamy. Season with pinch of salt.

Re-spray pan. Pour egg whites over base of pan and cook very gently until just set. Ease a spatula under the edges of the omelette to prevent sticking.

Place cooked filling on one side of omelette and fold over other side.

No-Check Drinks & Desserts

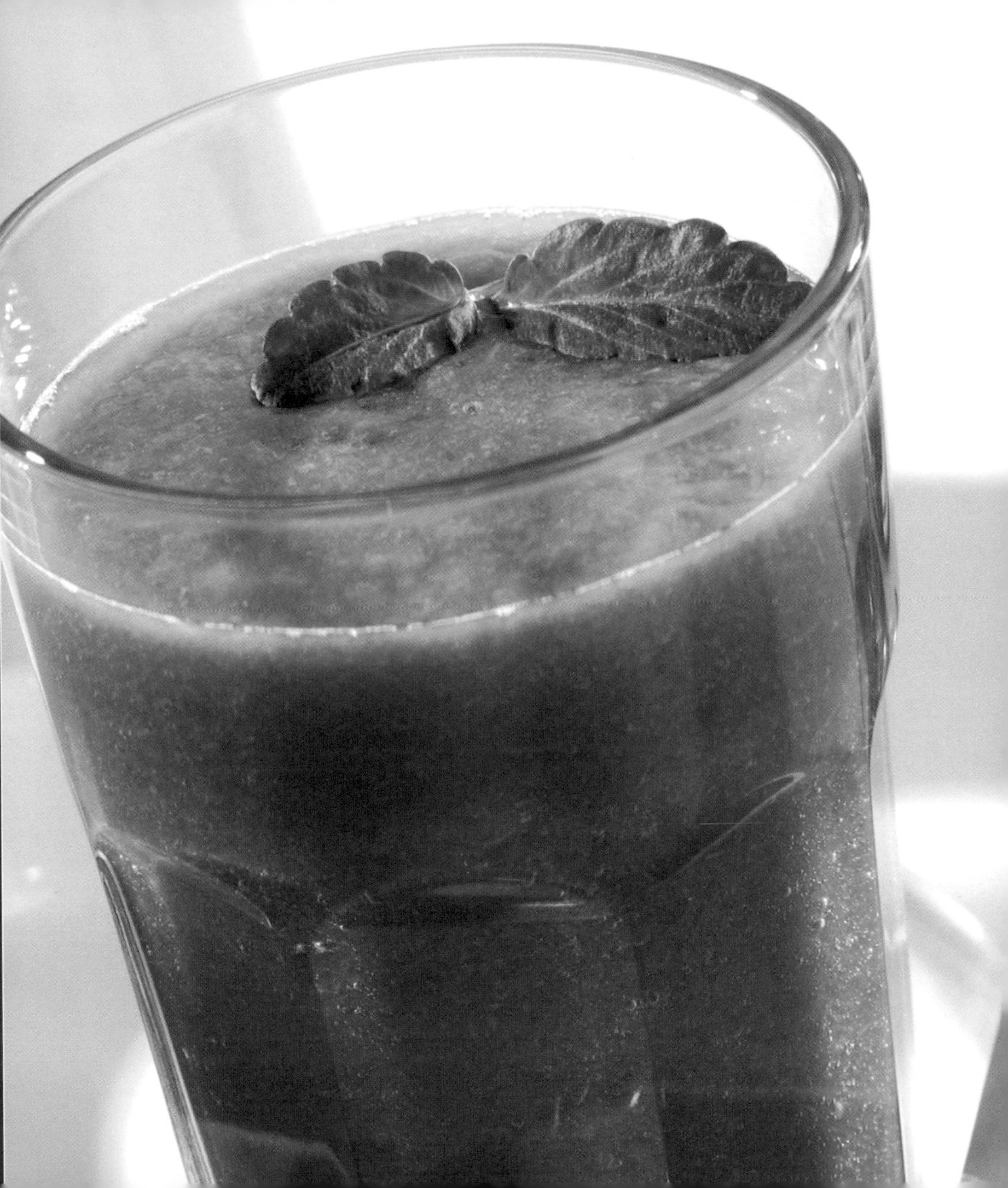

■ Rhubarb & Ginger Ale Smoothie

No-Check Food

• **150g/5 oz Hartley's No Added Sugar Solid Pack canned rhubarb***
• **1 tbsp granulated sweetener, or to taste**
• **150ml/¼ pint low-calorie American ginger ale**

Place rhubarb, sweetener and ginger ale in a blender and whizz until smooth.

* Alternatively, use fresh rhubarb that has been cooked either with the minimum amount of water and sweetener to taste, or in a little low-calorie orange squash.

■ Peach Smoothie

No-Check Food

using Every Day Bonus fruit* and milk*

• **2 large or 3 medium halves canned peaches in juice, drained**
• **150ml/¼ pint skimmed milk**
• **1-2 tsp granulated sweetener to taste**

Place peaches and milk in a blender and whizz until smooth. Stir in sweetener to taste.

* *Peaches are equivalent to 1 average serving Every Day Bonus fruit. Milk is equivalent to half Every Day Bonus allowance.*

If not using Every Day Bonus, count 2 Checks for peaches and 2 Checks for milk.

■ Mint Tea

Ideal if you have plenty of mint growing in the garden! Mint tea may help relieve flatulence and heartburn.

- **40g/1½ oz fresh mint leaves**
- **600ml/1 pint boiling water**

Wash and chop mint leaves, removing any tough stems as you go. Place in a heatproof container and pour on boiling water.

Cover and leave to infuse 10 minutes. Strain through a sieve. Dilute with additional boiling water if brew is too strong for your liking.

Tea will keep for 2 days in the fridge and can be gently re-heated.

■ Fresh Lemonade

- **1 large lemon**
- **600ml/1 pint ice-cold water**
- **1-2 tbsp granulated sweetener, or to taste**

Cut lemon in half and remove pips. Squeeze out all the juice and flesh into a jug (a lemon squeezer makes it easy!).

Pour on ice-cold water (or add 6 ice cubes and 450ml/¾ pint water). Stir in granulated sweetener to taste.

■ Sweet Spiced Squash

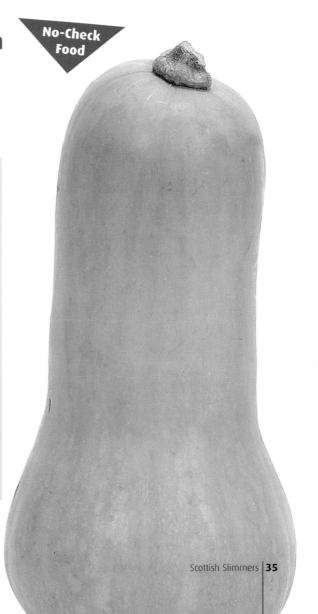

No-Check Food

- **900g/2 lb approx. butternut squash**
- **4 tbsp granulated sweetener, or to taste**
- **1 tsp cinnamon, or to taste**

Peel squash and remove seeds. Cut into chunks.

Boil in unsalted water until tender. Allow to cool a little, drain reserving the cooking liquid.

Place chunks in blender together with sweetener and cinnamon and blend in short bursts to a smooth, thick purée. Stir with a fork between bursts. Add a little of the cooking liquid if necessary, but take care as you don't want to end up with soup!

Makes around 4-6 servings.

For a treat, serve topped with an ice-cream-scoop-size swirl of half-fat aerosol cream. Count 1 Check 2g fat.

nb: This recipe has hints of American pumpkin pie. We've used butternut squash rather than pumpkin as it is more often available in the UK, but around Halloween time, you might want to try it using pumpkin.

■ Jelly Foam

- **1 sachet sugar-free jelly crystals, any flavour**
- **2 egg whites (see note below)**

Place jelly crystals in a bowl and pour on 300ml/½ pint boiling water. Stir thoroughly to dissolve. Stir in 150ml/¼ pint cold water. Allow to cool, but not set.

When jelly is cool, whisk egg whites in a large bowl to form stiff peaks. Start by stirring 2 tbsp jelly into the egg whites (not the other way round). Gradually add remaining jelly, stirring thoroughly. Egg whites should have jelly stirred into them, but will still float to the top.

Either level foam evenly over the top and leave to set, or spoon into 4-6 glasses or individual serving dishes ensuring foam is equally divided and levelled over the top before allowing to set.

 nb: This recipe contains raw egg white. Although Lion Quality eggs have been shown to be virtually salmonella-free, it is still recommended that pregnant women, babies and young children, the elderly or anyone with a compromised immune system should avoid raw or undercooked eggs.

■ Pink Cloud

- **150-175g/5-6 oz cooked rhubarb***
- **1 egg white**
- **1 dspn heat-stable granulated sweetener**

Pre-heat oven to hottest setting.

Put cooked rhubarb into an ovenproof dish. Whisk egg white until stiff. Fold in sweetener and spread over rhubarb.

Bake in hot oven 7-8 minutes until crisp and golden. Eat right away!

* Rhubarb should be cooked either with water and sweetener, or in a little low-calorie orange squash. Alternatively, Hartley's No Added Sugar, Solid Pack canned rhubarb may be used. Put required amount into dish and sprinkle with 1-2 tsp sweetener before covering with topping

Low on Checks and feel like a snack?
Each of the following ideas will cost you just one Check!

1 satsuma or tangerine	1	0
2 small plums	1	0
3 small semi-dried apricots	1	0
Freeze 40g/1½ oz grapes - suck slowly when frozen!	1	0
1 supermarket "fun-size" (children's lunchbox) apple	1	0
Stuff 1 tomato with 1 tbsp cottage cheese	1	1
Fill 25cm/10 inch stick of celery with 1 Laughing Cow Light Cheese Triangle - then cut into 10 pieces!	1	1
Top 1 Ryvita Original or Dark Rye Crispbread or 1 rice-cake with tomato/cucumber slices and/or a scraping of Marmite	1	0
Dip no-Check vegetable strips into 1 tbsp (about 25-30g/1 oz) Philadelphia Extra Light Soft Cheese or Sainsbury's Be Good To Yourself Low Fat Soft Cheese.	1	1
2 wafer-thin slices ham, chicken or turkey plus no-Check salad	1	1
2 shredded seafood sticks sprinkled with a few drops soy sauce plus no-Check salad	1	1
1 Wall's strawberry, chocolate or vanilla Mini Milk Lolly	1	1
Unlimited sugar-free jelly with 55ml (ice-cream scoop-size) swirl Anchor Light Aerosol Dairy Cream	1	2
60g/2 oz raspberries or chopped strawberries with 30ml/2 level tbsp Anchor Light Aerosol Dairy Cream	1	1
7g/about a handful Puffed Wheat	1	0
7g/about a handful Rice Krispies	1	0
1 rich tea finger biscuit	1	1
1 sponge finger	1	0
1 Doria Amaretti biscuit	1	0.5
1 Cremosa Chupa Chups Sugar-free Lolly	1	0.5

Low-Check Recipes

■ Sausages in Red Wine Gravy

per serving 150 6

Serves 1

- **2 Marks & Spencer Count On Us Sausages** *
- **1 small onion, sliced**
- **Spray oil**
- **½ Bovril cube**
- **100ml/3½ fl.oz hot water**
- **1 tsp tomato purée**
- **2 tbsp red wine**

Grill the sausages.

Cook onions slowly in pan sprayed with oil until soft and starting to brown. Add a little water if necessary to help soften and prevent sticking.

Dissolve stock cube in hot water.

Stir tomato purée into onions and cook 30 seconds. Add wine and allow to bubble up. Add stock and boil to reduce a little.

Add sausages to pan and simmer 2 minutes.

* Other brand very-low-calorie sausages may be used, up to 65 calories per sausage.

■ Normandy Pork

Serves 2

- **2 x 115g/4 oz pork escalopes**
- **1 small onion, sliced thinly**
- **1 small Cox's apple, cored and sliced**
- **Spray oil**
- **1 chicken Oxo cube**
- **100ml/3½ fl.oz hot water**
- **½ tsp mild mustard**
- **1 rounded tbsp fat-free fromage frais**

Beat out escalopes until ½ cm/¼ inch thick.

Cook onions gently in a non-stick pan sprayed with oil until soft and starting to colour. Add a little water if necessary to prevent sticking. Add apple slices and cook 5-7 minutes until softened and starting to colour, occasionally stirring and turning over apple slices. Remove from pan.

Re-spray pan and cook escalopes over moderate heat about 3 minutes each side, or until cooked through.

Dissolve stock cube in hot water.

Return apples and onions to pan with pork. Pour over stock and stir mustard in thoroughly. Simmer 2 minutes turning over escalopes now and again.

Remove pan from heat, tilt pan and stir fromage frais thoroughly into juices.

Serve half the recipe to each person.

■ Honey, Lemon & Garlic Turkey

per serving   150 6 1

Serves 1

- **115g/4 oz turkey breast**
- **1 tsp honey**
- **1 dspn lemon juice**
- **1 small clove garlic, crushed**
- **Salt**
- **Spray oil**

Cut turkey into 2 thin escalopes. If necessary, beat out to flatten

Mix together the honey, lemon and garlic in a shallow dish. Use to coat the escalopes and leave to marinate 15 minutes. Season lightly with salt.

Spray pan with oil and heat. Cook the escalopes over medium heat, approximately 1½ minutes each side, or until cooked through but not dried out.

■ Fisherman's Stew

per serving 75 3 1

Courtesy of Class Manager, Lorraine Queen

Serves 4

- **1 medium onion, chopped**
- **1 clove garlic, crushed**
- **Spray oil**
- **Pinch each of mixed herbs, oregano and chilli powder**
- **1 tbsp white wine**
- **1 fish stock cube**
- **600ml/1 pint hot water**
- **400g can chopped tomatoes**
- **2 tbsp tomato purée**
- **60g/2 oz carrots, diced**
- **2 small new potatoes, diced**
- **100g/3½ oz smoked whiting or smoked cod**
- **20g/¾ oz smoked salmon**
- **100g/3½ oz prawns, defrosted if frozen**

Soften onion and garlic in a saucepan sprayed with oil, over medium heat. Stir in herbs, chilli powder and wine and simmer gently 2 minutes.

Dissolve stock cube in hot water. Stir tomatoes and tomato purée into saucepan, followed by the stock, potatoes and carrots. Simmer 15 minutes, stirring now and again.

Microwave the smoked whiting or cod 1 minute, then flake gently with your fingertips to ensure any bones are removed. Add to saucepan together with the smoked salmon. Simmer 5 minutes, add the prawns and simmer a further 5 minutes.

Serve one-quarter of the recipe to each person.

■ Vegetable & Pasta Lunch Bowl

per serving   70   3 0

Courtesy of member Sandra Almond, Accrington

Serves 4

- 1 onion, chopped
- 1 leek, sliced
- 1 stick celery, chopped
- 2 carrots, diced
- 2 cloves garlic, crushed
- 600ml/1 pint chicken stock
- 200g canned chopped tomatoes
- 60g/2 oz frozen peas
- 60g/2 oz soup pasta
- 1 tsp caster sugar
- 1dspn dried parsley
- 1 dspn dried basil
- Salt and pepper

Put onion, leek, celery, carrots and garlic into a large saucepan and add chicken stock. Bring to the boil, then simmer 10 minutes.

Add tomatoes and peas and bring back to the boil. Add pasta, sugar, herbs and seasoning to taste. Simmer until pasta is tender, stirring now and again.

Serve one-quarter of the recipe to each person.

■ Pasta Brunch

per serving   150 **6** 2

Serves 1

- **30g/1 oz pasta shapes**
- **Spray oil**
- **1 small onion, chopped**
- **2 turkey rashers, chopped**
- **1 tomato, chopped**
- **2-3 mushrooms, sliced**

Cook pasta in lightly salted boiling water until just tender.

Spray pan with oil and cook onions until softened. Add chopped turkey rashers, mushrooms and tomatoes and cook until browned.

Drain pasta and stir into turkey mixture.

■ Orange & Soy Quorn Fillets

per serving   150 6 2

Serves 1

- **2 frozen Quorn Fillets (uncoated)**
- **75ml/5 tbsp unsweetened orange juice**
- **1 tsp soy sauce**
- **½ tsp granulated sweetener**
- **½ tsp cornflour**
- **A few finely chopped mint leaves (optional)**

Place fillets, orange juice and soy sauce in a small pan and heat gently until completely thawed and warmed through. Turn fillets frequently.

Remove fillets to serving dish.

Stir sweetener into juice. Mix cornflour with 1 tbsp water and stir thoroughly into juice approximately 20 seconds.

If using, stir chopped mint into sauce. Pour sauce over fillets.

■ Vegetable Spring Rolls

per roll   75   **3** ①

- **2 spring onions, sliced**
- **60g/2 oz frozen sliced mixed peppers**
- **Spray oil**
- **1 small carrot, peeled and coarsely grated**
- **1 tbsp frozen peas**
- **85g/3 oz beansprouts**
- **½ Oxo Chinese cube**
- **2 x 45g large sheets filo pastry (e.g. Jus-rol)**

Pre-heat oven to 200°C/gas mark 6.

Cook onions and peppers in pan sprayed with oil approximately 3 minutes. Stir in grated carrot, peas, beansprouts and crumbled ½ Chinese cube. Stir-fry 1 minute. Remove from heat.

Lay 1 filo sheet on flat surface and spray top side with oil. Place other sheet on top and cut, down and across, into 4 rectangles.

Put quarter of the vegetable mixture at the short end of each piece of pastry. Roll up each piece, tucking in sides.

Place rolls on a non-stick baking tray and spray lightly with oil. Bake approximately 20 minutes, until golden.

■ Corned Beef & Hoisin Wrappers

per serving 150 6 (5)

Serves 1

- **5cm/2" piece of cucumber**
- **1 spring onion**
- **50g/1¾ oz Princes Lean Corned Beef**
- **A few lettuce leaves, preferably cos, Romaine or Little Gem**
- **2 rounded tsp, hoisin or plum sauce**

Cut the cucumber into strips. Cut the spring onion lengthways into strips. Cut the corned beef into small cubes.

Arrange all the ingredients on a plate. Take a lettuce leaf, place on some spring onion and cucumber, then some corned beef and a dab or two of sauce. Wrap lettuce around the filling and eat.

Continue until everything is eaten!

■ Spanish Tuna Salad

per serving   150   6   7

Serves 2

Courtesy of Class Assistant Jaqui McIntosh, Edinburgh

- **1 small carrot, chopped**
- **1 red pepper, de-seeded and chopped into chunks**
- **1 tbsp frozen peas**
- **1 hard-boiled egg, cooled and chopped**
- **85-100g can tuna in brine, drained**
- **60g/2 oz cooked prawns or seafood mix, defrosted if frozen**
- **2 tbsp low-calorie mayonnaise**
- **1 clove garlic, finely chopped.**

Cook carrot in boiling water. When almost tender, add peppers and peas and cook 2 minutes. Drain and cool.

Mix vegetables with chopped egg, flaked tuna and prawns.

Mix mayonnaise with garlic and stir through salad mixture.

Serve half the recipe to each person.

Low-Check Main Meals

■ Red Pesto Chicken with Pan-fried Courgettes & New Potatoes

Serves 1

- **1 medium skinless chicken breast**
- **1 button mushroom, finely chopped**
- **1 level dspn red pesto (e.g. Bertolli Pesto Rosso)**
- **1 turkey rasher**
- **150g/5 oz new potatoes, boiled**
- **1 medium courgette, sliced**
- **Spray oil**

Pre-heat oven to 180°C/gas mark 4.

Cut chicken breast horizontally almost in half and open out like a book. Place chopped mushrooms and pesto on one side and fold over other side to cover.

Wrap turkey rasher around chicken breast and secure with 1 or 2 cocktail sticks. Place in a shallow ovenproof dish and bake, uncovered 25 minutes, until cooked through.

Meanwhile, cut boiled new potatoes in half. Spray pan with oil and heat. Place potatoes on one side of pan, cut side down, and spread courgette slices over remaining base of pan. Cook over medium heat until browned underneath. Turn over potatoes and courgettes and brown other side.

Remove cocktail stick from chicken and serve with potatoes and courgettes.

■ Microwave Meatloaf & Mash

Serves 4

- **75g/2½ oz small onion, chopped**
- **75g/2½ oz carrot, coarsely grated**
- **400g/14 oz lean minced beef**
- **1 dspn Worcester sauce**
- **1 dspn tomato purée**
- **1 dspn dried parsley**
- **2 Bovril cubes**
- **1 egg, beaten**
- **600g/1¼ lb potatoes**
- **4 dspn low-fat gravy granules (e.g. Oxo or Bisto Best)**
- **No-Check vegetables to serve**

Peel and boil potatoes and when cooked mash with some of the cooking liquid.

Place onions and carrots in a 1 litre/2 pint microwavable, covered casserole dish. Microwave on high 3½-4 minutes or until soft. Mix in mince, Worcester sauce, tomato purée and parsley. Crumble in stock cubes, add beaten egg and mix thoroughly. Press down mixture and cover.

Microwave on medium (approximately 500 watts) 12 minutes. Stand 5 minutes, then drain off surplus fat.

Make up gravy with 300ml/½ pint boiling water.

Serve one-quarter of the meatloaf, potatoes and gravy to each person with your choice of no-Check vegetables.

 nb: The meatloaf is also good eaten cold with salad.

One-quarter of the loaf alone is   175   **7**

■ Beef Chow Mein

per serving   310 **12** ⑥

Serves 2

- **175g/6 oz lean steak, e.g. rump**
- **4 spring onions**
- **Spray oil**
- **150g/5 oz beansprouts**
- **Handful of shredded savoy cabbage, pak choi or other greens**
- **150g pack Amoy Straight to Wok Noodles**
- **120g sachet Blue Dragon Chow Mein Sauce**

Cut the steak into small, thin strips. Slice the spring onions diagonally.

Spray pan or wok with oil and heat. Add the steak and spring onions and stir-fry 2 minutes.

Add the beansprouts, greens and noodles and stir 1 minute, separating the noodles. Add sauce and stir 1 minute more.

Serve half to each person.

■ Tagliatelle with Ham, Peas & Crème Fraîche

per serving　　　　　　　　　　　　　　　　　　300　**12**　⑦

Serves 1

- **45g/1½ oz tagliatelle or pasta shapes**
- **2 rounded tbsp frozen peas**
- **45g/1½ oz lean smoked ham, chopped**
- **2 level tbsp half-fat crème fraîche**
- **Black pepper**

Cook pasta in lightly salted boiling water until just tender. Add peas to water about 3 minutes before end of cooking time.

Drain pasta and peas and return to pan. Stir in ham and crème fraîche and warm through gently a few seconds, stirring continuously.

Season to taste with black pepper.

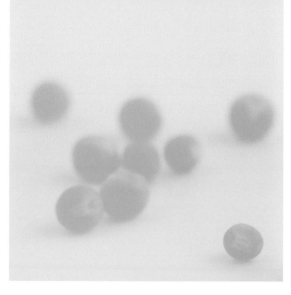

■ Chicken & Potato Curry

per serving   310   **12** (10)

Serves 2

- **2 medium skinless chicken breasts**
- **1 onion, sliced**
- **Spray oil**
- **2 level tbsp Korma curry paste (e.g. Patak's)**
- **200g/7 oz peeled weight potatoes, cut into 20 cubes**
- **400g can tomatoes**
- **150g/5 oz frozen spinach**
- **Garam masala (optional)**

Cut chicken breasts into cubes. Spray a large saucepan with oil and stir-fry chicken and onions over high heat about 7 minutes.

Stir in curry paste and cubed potatoes and stir 1 minute more.

Stir in tomatoes and spinach. Bring to the boil, then turn down heat, cover and simmer gently approximately 30 minutes. Stir frequently, breaking up tomatoes and spinach, until potatoes are cooked.

Serve half the recipe to each person and sprinkle with a little garam masala (optional).

■ Top Tapas

total for all 3 recipes   270 **11** 10

Serves 1

Courtesy of Class Assistant Jaqui McIntosh, Edinburgh

Ideally, each recipe should be served in a separate small tapas dish - but they're equally delicious served on a plate!

Gambas al Ajillo (Garlic Prawns)   80 **3** 2

- **½ tsp olive oil**
- **60g/2 oz prawns**
- **1 clove garlic, finely chopped**

Heat oil in a pan, add prawns and garlic and stir-fry 2 minutes.

Patatas Bravas (Spicy Potatoes)   150 **6** 4

- **100g McCain home roasts**
- **1 dspn tomato ketchup**
- **Dash of hot chilli sauce**

Oven-bake potatoes as directed. Mix tomato ketchup with chilli sauce and spoon over potatoes.

Ensalada de pimientos rojos (Red Pepper Salad)   40 **2** 4

- **1 small red pepper, de-seeded and chopped into chunks**
- **1 plum tomato, chopped into chunks**
- **1 tsp olive oil**
- **Dash of white wine vinegar**

Mix all ingredients together.

■ Steamed Sweet Chilli Fish & Noodles

per serving   280   11 ③

Serves 2

- **150g pack Amoy Straight to Wok Noodles**
- **300g/10 oz skinless cod or other white fish, defrosted if frozen**
- **2 spring onions, finely sliced**
- **2 tbsp sweet chilli sauce**
- **No-Check vegetables to serve**

Cut 2 large squares of strong foil. Put half the noodles on each piece of foil, spreading them out a little.

Cut the fish into chunks and place on top of the noodles together with the spring onions.

Top each portion with 1 tbsp sweet chilli sauce, then scrunch up the foil to make 2 well-sealed parcels. Take care not to puncture foil.

Bring 5cm/2 inches water to the boil in a pan large enough to take the two parcels. Place parcels in water, keep at a gentle boil and cook approximately 8 minutes. Remove parcels with a slotted spoon, open carefully and transfer noodles and fish onto 2 serving plates.

Serve with no-Check vegetables, either boiled, microwaved, or stir-fried in spray oil.

■ Fish & Prawn Pie

per serving   300 **12** 7

Serves 1

- **200g/7 oz potato**
- **85g/3 oz broccoli**
- **150g pack Ross Fish Choice Fish in Butter Sauce**
- **30g/1 oz cooked prawns, defrosted if frozen**

Boil potato. Drain, leaving a little water in the pan, then mash.

Boil or microwave broccoli, drain and chop.

Boil or microwave fish in sauce according to pack instructions.

In a grill-proof dish, mix chopped broccoli with prawns and fish in sauce. Top with mashed potato and brown under the grill.

■ Spicy Chickpeas & Couscous

Serves 1

- **1 small onion, chopped**
- **Spray oil**
- **1 clove garlic, crushed**
- **Pinch cumin**
- **Pinch cinnamon**
- **½ tsp turmeric**
- **1 small carrot, sliced thinly**
- **200ml/7 fl.oz chicken or vegetable stock**
- **1 courgette, sliced**
- **1 tomato, chopped**
- **4 ready-to-eat apricots, halved**
- **4 tbsp canned chickpeas**
- **45g/1½ oz couscous**

Soften onion in a medium saucepan sprayed with oil. Add garlic and spices and cook 1 minute stirring. Add carrots and stock, bring back to a simmer, cover and cook 10 minutes, checking occasionally.

Add courgettes, tomatoes, apricots and chickpeas. Bring back to a simmer and cook 5-10 minutes covered, stirring now and again, until courgettes are just tender.

Push vegetables to one side of the pan and stir couscous into juices. Cover, remove from heat and allow to stand 5 minutes.

Fluff couscous with a fork before serving. If dish is too dry, stir in a little boiling water.

Low-Check Sweet Treats

■ Quick Strawberry Trifle

per serving   160 **6**

Serves 1

- **1 trifle sponge**
- **50g/about 4-5 strawberries, quartered**
- **1 tsp granulated sweetener**
- **125g pot diet strawberry yoghurt**

Cut trifle sponge into 8 small cubes.

Sprinkle the strawberries with the sweetener and leave 10 minutes.

Put half the sponge and half the strawberries into a glass or serving dish. Top with one-third of the yoghurt.

Repeat with remaining ingredients, using all remaining yoghurt and reserving 1 piece of strawberry for decoration.

■ Ambassador's Choice

per piece   35 **1.5**

Makes 24

- **8 Ryvita Multigrain crispbreads**
- **100g/3½ oz chocolate hazelnut spread**

Put Ryvitas into a polythene bag and crush quite finely.

Melt chocolate spread in a bowl over a pan of simmering water. Remove bowl from heat and stir in crushed Ryvita crumbs.

Take a teaspoonful of the mixture, pat gently into a ball and place in a paper sweet case. Repeat to make 24.

■ Brandied Apricots

per serving		80	3	0
or using 1 average serving of fruit from Every Day Bonus		20	1	0

- **411g can apricot halves in fruit juice**
- **Zest from ½ a small unwaxed lemon**
- **1 dspn lemon juice**
- **1-2 tbsp granulated sweetener**
- **2 tbsp brandy or cream sherry**

Place apricots with fruit juice, lemon zest and lemon juice into a saucepan. Heat through. Use a slotted spoon to remove apricots. Keep warm.

Boil juices 2 minutes to reduce. Remove pan from heat and allow to come off the boil. Stir in granulated sweetener thoroughly, then stir in brandy or sherry. Pour juice over apricots. Best served warm.

Serve one-third of the recipe to each person

■ Honeyed Figs

per serving		70	3	0
or using 1 average serving of fruit from Every Day Bonus		20	1	0

Serves 1

- **2 fresh figs**
- **1 tsp runny honey**

Cut figs in half from stalk to base.

Place on grill rack and drizzle with honey.

Grill under moderate heat until fruits soften and honey bubbles.

■ Apple Snow

per serving 50

or using 1 average serving of fruit from Every Day Bonus

No-Check

Serves 2

- **300g/10 oz cooking apples, peeled, cored and chopped**
- **2 tbsp water**
- **2 tbsp granulated sweetener, or to taste**
- **2 medium egg whites (see note below)**

Gently stew the apples in the water, or microwave in a suitable covered dish, until soft. Allow to cool.

Add the sweetener, transfer to a blender and whizz until smooth. Turn out into a large bowl using a spatula to scrape down the sides of the blender.

Beat egg whites until they stand up in peaks and fold gently into the apples using a metal spoon.

Divide between 2 serving dishes.

Variations

Top each serving with 1 swirl (about the size of an ice cream scoop) half-fat aerosol dairy cream.
Per serving, add 25

or

Top each serving with cream as above, plus 1 tsp chocolate vermicelli
Per serving, add 45

 nb: This recipe contains raw egg white. Although Lion Quality eggs have been shown to be virtually salmonella-free, it is still recommended that pregnant women, babies and young children, the elderly or anyone with a compromised immune system should avoid raw or undercooked eggs.

■ Jelly with Orange Cream

per serving   50 **2** (0)

Serves 4

- **1 sachet sugar-free orange jelly crystals**
- **250g tub quark skimmed milk soft cheese**
- **2 tbsp granulated sweetener (or to taste)**
- **2-3 drops vanilla essence or extract**
- **Juice from ½ orange**
- **Finely grated/zested peel from ½ orange (no pith)**

Dissolve jelly crystals in 275ml/½ pint boiling water, then make up to 550ml/1 pint with cold water. Allow to cool, but not to set.

When cool, pour jelly into 4 serving glasses or dishes. Put in a cool place to set jelly.

Lightly beat quark and thoroughly mix in the sweetener, vanilla, orange juice and half the orange zest.

Divide the mixture between the 4 jellies, putting a large swirl on each, and decorate with remaining zest.

If preparing in advance, make up jellies and orange cream separately. Stir cream and put onto jellies just before serving.

■ Alaska Special

per serving 130 **5** (3)

Serves 4

- **2 large egg whites**
- **3 tbsp heat-stable granulated sweetener (e.g. Splenda)**
- **1 medium banana, thinly sliced**
- **500ml tub, or half of 1 litre tub, low-calorie ice cream in chocolate and/or vanilla flavour (e.g. Carte d'Or Light)**
- **1 tbsp brandy or cream sherry**

Pre-heat oven to 220°C/gas mark 8.

Whisk egg whites to form stiff peaks. Fold in granulated sweetener.

Spread banana slices over the base of an ovenproof plate. Place ice cream on top of banana.

With a small sharp knife, make a few deep slits in the top of the ice cream and sprinkle in the brandy or cream sherry.

Cover ice cream completely with egg white, making sure it is completely sealed. Don't worry if the odd banana slice pokes out, but there shouldn't be any gaps over the ice cream.

Place in hot oven and cook approximately 4-5 minutes, until meringue is golden. Serve immediately.

Serve one-quarter of the recipe to each person.

■ Prune & Apple Muffins

per muffin 150 6 4

Makes 10

- **100g/3½ oz self-raising white flour**
- **100g/3½ oz self-raising wholemeal flour**
- **½ tsp baking powder**
- **2 tbsp heat-stable granulated sweetener (e.g. Splenda)**
- **40g/1½ oz sugar**
- **175ml/6 fl.oz skimmed milk**
- **2 medium eggs**
- **2 tbsp sunflower or vegetable oil**
- **1 apple, peeled and diced**
- **60g/2 oz ready-to-eat prunes, chopped**

Pre-heat oven to 200°C/gas mark 6.

Place 10 muffin cases in a muffin pan or deep bun tin, or on a baking tray (but they won't hold their shape as well if not supported at the sides).

Sift the flours, baking powder and sweetener into a bowl, then stir in the wholemeal bran left in the sieve. Stir in the sugar.

Beat the milk, eggs and oil together well. Make a well in the flour and pour in the liquid. Beat lightly until just mixed. Do not over-beat. Fold in the apples and prunes and spoon mixture into the muffin cases.

Bake approximately 25 minutes until well risen. Put muffins on a wire rack to cool. (If you peel off the paper case too soon, half the muffin will stick to the bottom!).

Best eaten the same day, but can be frozen. Either allow to defrost about 1 hour, or pop frozen muffin in the microwave around 30-45 seconds.

■ Sultana Scones

Makes 12

- **225g/8 oz plain flour**
- **Pinch of salt**
- **1 tsp baking powder**
- **100g/3½ oz low-fat spread**
- **2 level tbsp sugar**
- **30g/1 oz sultanas**
- **1 medium egg**
- **3 tbsp skimmed milk**
- **Skimmed milk to glaze**

Pre-heat oven to 200°C/gas mark 6.

Sift flour, salt and baking powder into a bowl. Rub in the low-fat spread until it resembles breadcrumbs. Stir in the sugar and sultanas.

Beat the egg with the 3 tbsp milk. Gradually add to the dry mixture and mix to a soft dough.

Turn out onto a lightly floured surface and roll out to 1cm/½ inch thickness. Cut out 12 rounds using a 5cm/2 inch cutter and place on a lightly oil-sprayed baking sheet. Alternatively, cover baking sheet with non-stick foil (e.g. BacoFoil Release).

Brush the tops with a little skimmed milk and bake approximately 15-20 minutes until a light golden colour. Transfer to a wire rack to cool.

■ No-Added-Fat Sponge

per serving 145 6 2

Serves 8

- **2 medium eggs**
- **115g/4 oz caster sugar**
- **115g/4 oz self-raising flour**
- **5 level tbsp reduced-sugar jam**
- **1 tsp icing sugar**

Pre-heat oven to 180°C/gas mark 4.

Line a 20cm/8 inch loose-bottom cake tin with non-stick foil (e.g. BacoFoil Release).

Put eggs and sugar into a bowl and with an electric whisk, whisk until pale, thick and creamy.

Sift flour into the bowl and fold into eggs and sugar mix. Turn mix into the cake tin and bake just above centre of oven approximately 30 minutes or until firm to the touch.

Leave in tin 5 minutes, then turn out onto a wire rack to cool.

Split sponge horizontally through the centre and spread with the reduced-sugar jam. Sift icing sugar over the top.

nb: nb: Unfilled sponge can be used as the base for fruit-filled or topped gateaux, or just served with fruit and/or ice cream. (Add Checks as appropriate.)

Sponge alone, per one-eighth serving

125 5 2

No-Check Food Lists

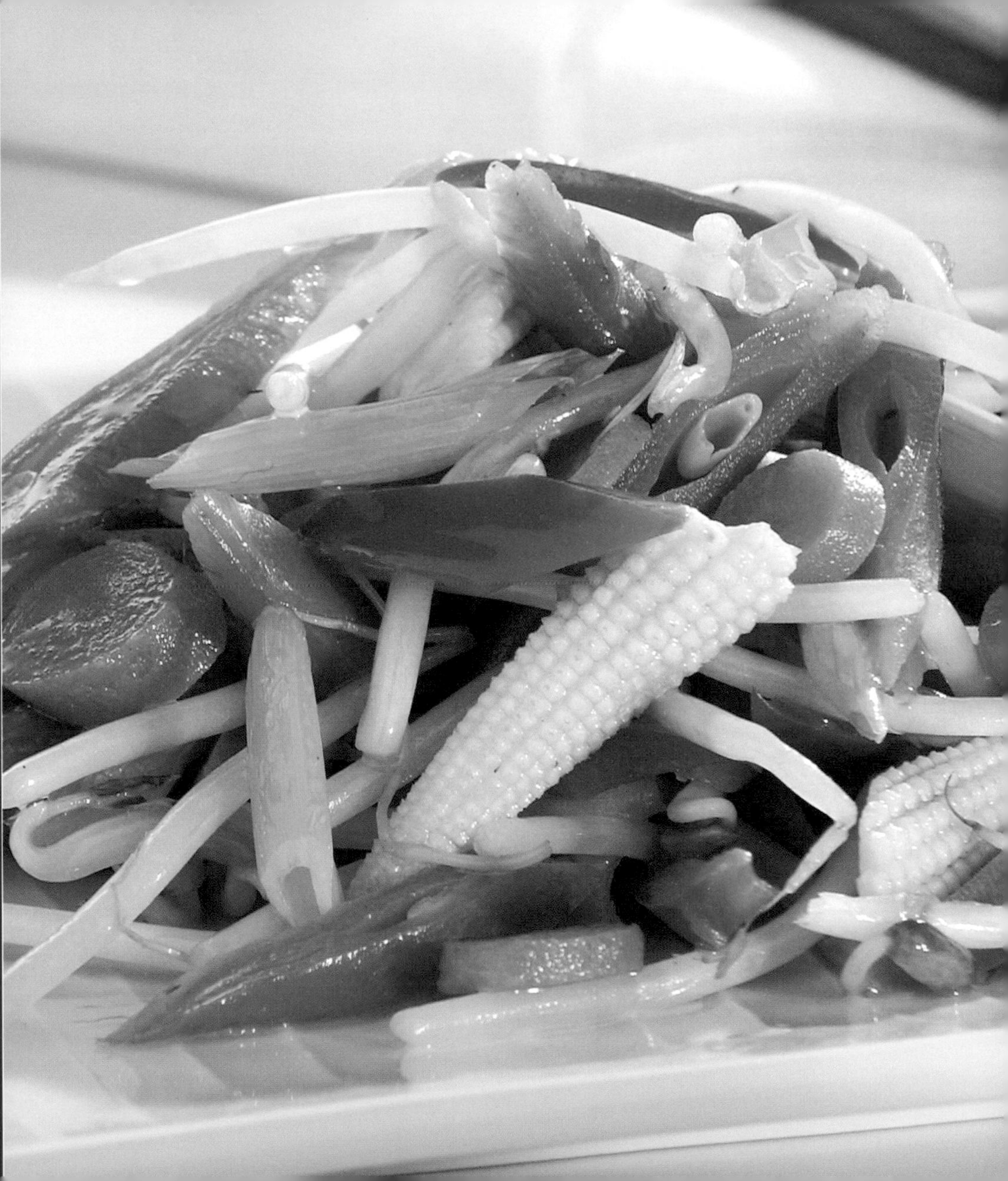

USING No-Check Vegetables

The vegetables listed on the following pages have No-Check value so may be used freely on the Positive Eating Plan.

Use to make :
soups
salads
vegetable purées
sauces
in stews and casseroles
in stir-fries
or finely chopped to extend mince

They may be :
eaten raw
boiled
steamed
poached in stock
or microwaved

Or, using a few sprays of low-calorie spray oil, they may be :
pan-fried
roasted
grilled
or barbecue

No-Check

Tip

For good health choose vegetables in a variety of colours.

Tip

Vegetables may be fresh or frozen. If choosing canned, ideally go for low or reduced salt varieties.

Alfalfa sprouts

Artichoke hearts

Asparagus

Aubergine

Baby sweetcorn

Bamboo shoots

Beansprouts

Beetroot

Bok choi/pak choi

Broccoli

Brussels sprouts

Cabbage, all types

Calabrese

Carrots

Cauliflower

Celeriac

Celery

Chard

Chicory

Chinese leaves

Christophene (cho-cho)

Courgettes

Cress

Cucumber

Dandelion leaves

Endive

Fennel

French beans (haricots verts)

Green beans

Hearts of palm

Jerusalem artichokes

Kale

Khol rabi

Leeks

Vegetables

Lettuce, all types

Lotus tubers

Mangetout/snow peas

Marrow

Mooli

Mushrooms, all types including exotic

Okra

Onions, all types

Patty pan

Peppers, all colours

Pumpkin

Radishes

Runner beans

Salad leaves, all types

Salsify

Seaweed (not deep fried)

Shallots

Spinach

Spring greens

Squash, all types, e.g. acorn, butternut

Sugar snap peas

Swede

Tomatoes

Turnips

Water chestnuts

Watercress

No-Check Additions

Artificial sweeteners

Baking powder *

Beef extract *

Chilli peppers

Cream of tartar

Dried vegetables

Egg white

Essences & extracts, e.g. vanilla

Garlic

Gelatine

Herbs, fresh, frozen or dried

Orange flower water

Rhubarb

Root ginger

Rose water

Spices, whole or powdered

Stock cubes*/Stock granules*/Bouillon*

Sundried tomatoes (not in oil)

Tomato purée (no added oil)

Spray cooking oil

Sugar-free gum

Sugar-free jelly

Vegetarian gelling powder

Yeast, fresh or dried

Yeast extract*

No-Check Drinks

Water

Bottled waters up to 3 calories per 100ml

Teas, china or indian

Teas, fruit or herbal

Diet fizzy drinks up to 3 calories per 100ml

Diet mixers

No-added-sugar low-calorie squashes